Speed Networking

Five Simple Steps to Sell Your Products and Services

Cynthia D. Martin

Top-Ranked Sales Expert

Copyright © 2017 by Cynthia D. Martin

All rights reserved. No part of this book may be reproduced, stored in a retrieval system, or transmitted by any form or by any means, electronic, mechanical, photocopying, recording, or otherwise, except as may be expressly permitted by the applicable copyright statuses or in writing by the Publisher.

The author is not responsible for any results that you may or may not get from reading and implementing this material. Just remember that when you work towards being good at what matters to you, something good will happen.

Manufactured in the United States of America.

Published by:
GBM Enterprises, LLC.

For information contact:
Cynthia D. Martin
Cynthia@DCSpeedNetworking.com

ISBN: 978-0-9985560-0-0

Library of Congress Control Number: 2017900114

Cover and Interior Design by Jessica Tilles/TWA Solutions.com

TABLE OF CONTENTS

Dedication v
About the Author vii
How to Use This Book for Speed Networking xi
Foreword xiii

Introduction 1

Chapter One: Networking Is For You 7
    It's Not Just For Job Seekers 7
    What's The Difference? 9
    What Is Your Clear Vision For Yourself? 11

Chapter Two: The Basis For The 5-Step Speed
    Networking Method 13
    Double Meaning Of Speed Networking 14
    A Deeper Look At Networking 16
    Innovative Networking With The 5-Step Speed
        Networking Method 18
    How Can You Reshape Networking? 20

Chapter Three: Step 1—I AM 22
    Creating Your "I AM" 25

Chapter Four: Step 2 —What Do I Do? 30
    Exploring Transformation, Change and Improvement 32

Chapter Five: Step 3—Why I Do This 39
    Beyond The Thirty Second Pitch 48

Chapter Six: Step 4—Add Value 51

Chapter Seven: Step 5—My Contact Information 57

Chapter Eight: The Finished Product 64
    The Script In One Continuous Narrative 64
    Your Words Are Your Way 66

Acknowledgments 68

Workbook 71

I dedicate this book to first-time entrepreneurs and people with side hustles who are ready to use powerful words to sell their products or services.

ABOUT THE AUTHOR

Cynthia D. Martin is a graduate of the University of North Carolina at Chapel Hill. She enjoys teaching, writing, and inspiring people to do exactly what brings them joy. She is a top-ranked sales expert with seventeen years of professional sales experience in the pharmaceutical and medical sales industry. Her passion is building strong client relationships that lead to collaborative wins for everyone involved.

She founded DC Speed Networking to teach others how to use powerful words to sell your products and services. She teaches her 5-Step Speed Networking Method at conferences and seminars.

Cynthia hosts and facilitates speed networking events for Sales organizations, entrepreneurs, side hustlers, and small business owners throughout the Washington, DC metropolitan area.

She is also co-partner with The Comprehensive Dental Continuum, LLC where she creates, develops, and executes the marketing and sales strategies for the company.

Cynthia is the mother of two daughters and a dog.

"Before you can make a connection with someone else, you will need to make a deep connection with yourself."

—Cynthia D. Martin

HOW TO USE THIS BOOK FOR SPEED NETWORKING

1. After reading each of the five steps, think deeply about your answers.
2. Write out your answers to the five steps repeatedly until each is concise and feels genuine to you.
3. Speak your answers into the mirror daily.
4. Use your new networking skills in a meaningful way every day.
5. Begin using the five steps out of sequence and in any social setting or print media.

Foreword

Cynthia and I professionally clicked the moment I met her at an entrepreneurial business conference. She approached me after my keynote address with a confidence and friendliness that many people fail to exude when meeting someone new. Her posture, body language and smile made me think she worked either in marketing, sales, or communications. We hit it off immediately and I wasn't surprised to hear that she had developed a new, innovative method she called, "speed networking." Since networking is my passion, I was curious to hear more. During our conversation, Cynthia asked authentic, focused questions about my thirty-year career as an author, the CEO of FraserNet, Inc., and founder of the PowerNetworking Conference. By the end of our conversation, she pledged support to my work and committed to attending one of my upcoming conferences.

I later realized, that in those few short minutes, Cynthia had taken our conversation through her 5 Step Speed

Networking Method. By adding "speed" to the networking process, she has created a new formula that boils down networking to its essential elements and allows individuals to instantly connect. In this book, *Speed Networking: Five Simple Steps to Sell Your Products and Services*, she richly dissects and explains the networking process throughout her informative and thought-provoking methods.

Networking is one of the means to attain a goal, whether long or short-term. As you will read in this book, Cynthia clearly understands the importance of giving added value in every exchange and interaction. Sharing knowledge is not giving up wealth and power but actually a way of getting it. Instead of focusing on you, focus on others. Do good for others and good follows you. How, you may ask, do you do that? This book will take you through those steps and transform the way you think about connecting with others. Instead of entering rambling conversations without focus, you will now know the key methods to creating authentic and mutually beneficial relationships.

Cynthia has taken networking one step further by specifically concentrating on individuals who have a product or service and those thinking about beginning a business. By being an entrepreneur (or contemplating it), you have already begun to take risks and seize new opportunities. The next step is to bring it to life by creating engaging, powerful sound bites

Foreword

about your entrepreneurial world. The information, ideas and resources within this pithy book helps you build rapport and allows your products and services to sell themselves. With Cynthia's successful background in sales, the book is peppered with marketing strategies and sales tips that you can seamlessly incorporate into your networking experience. Cynthia pulls you in to examine who you are and who you want to become. You are encouraged to answer compelling questions about yourself and your business that will prepare you for effective and stimulating networking.

Her exercises and workbook are some of the best learning tools I have seen to transform you from a mere attendee to a master networker. What makes this book so practical is that she gives you a formula to build a networking dialogue that can be used anywhere and in everyday situations. The innovations she has added to traditional networking can be built upon through her website, seminars and replicable speed networking events but this concise yet powerful book lays the foundation for you to network your way to success.

George C. Fraser
CEO, FraserNet, Inc.
Founder, PowerNetworking Conference

INTRODUCTION

Are People Really Listening?
Do Your Words Have Value?

Silence took over me. Words escaped me. I couldn't speak. I was standing face-to-face with an important client physician who was waiting for me to start my presentation. My six-foot-three manager was glaring at me. My trembling hands were clenching my sales materials. I was nervous and I had no words coming out of my opened mouth.

Have you ever found yourself in a similar situation? Have you avoided social events because you think you have nothing to say?

To be great at anything takes dedicated time for daily practice. Great leaders all over the globe have one commonality: they practice what makes them exceptionally great.

Speed Networking

I am a side hustler with a corporate job. By profession, I am in pharmaceutical and medical sales. To build powerful relationships, I must speak powerful words. My income potential depends on it. Many years ago, I quickly learned that I had to practice using words to keep my profits flowing. I never wanted to feel that nervous again.

Meaningful words must evoke images and carve out a space to live in the minds of consumers. Medical products need to solve problems and provide solutions for physicians and their patients. My selling efforts must be strong enough so the physician will remember the information when needed the most.

Thriving in a competitive industry for seventeen years required me to become better than most at selling. I wanted to win sales awards and receive recognition for my accomplishments as often as possible. Creating short, yet meaningful, conversations that resonated was the key to my successes. I received clinical data to present to physicians, but the words I used to relay that data were my own.

I chose powerful words and spoke in short sentences to create compelling stories around the clinical data and scientific outcomes. Physicians and nurses would respond positively to my method of conveying clinical information, saying, "I like the way you said that. I can definitely use your product for my patients." For years, I used my communication

Introduction

method, combined with the latest sales techniques, and collected the most prestigious sales awards, year after year.

I stumbled into creating my communication method and my own sales technique through observing other sales representatives who would "show up and throw up" in front of physicians, talking excessively about the product and never pausing to breathe, nor ask the physician a question. I've witnessed a physician walk away from a representative, start writing in a patient's chart and pretending to be distracted. To avoid being treated like a talking bobble head, I quickly developed a sales technique that has allowed me to build winning sales territories and outperform my colleagues.

Ongoing practice is important to maintain skills and develop habits that get great results. Every three months, my colleagues and I gather for three, intense days. We diligently practice our sales calls. We practice how to answer anticipated questions about our products from our clients. We study our products as if they are new to us. We discuss innovative win-win sales strategies to execute with our customers. Consistency breeds momentum.

Most of my colleagues have been in the pharmaceutical and medical sales industry for over a decade. Longevity doesn't necessarily matter. The willingness to exist in a perpetual learning mode is what matters. To continue to discover new ways to grow our ever-changing businesses is what matters. Networking with medical associations, hospital leaders, healthcare providers, as well as consumers, helps the industry develop targeted products that provide solutions to meet medical needs.

You may be a new entrepreneur, a seasoned entrepreneur, or *side*preneur with a side hustle, like me. Your commitment to any level of entrepreneurship means you bear the ultimate responsibility for creating structures and systems to support the growth of your business, but there is one important method you must learn when it comes to building your business: *speed networking*.

Networking is a dynamic form of marketing that I encourage you to do as often as possible. Your goals during networking will be to acquire new customers, retain loyal customers, and provide value to everyone you meet.

Ninety percent of your success is marketing you and your business. Marketing has an enormous price tag, but networking is *free*.

I wrote this book to teach you how to combine networking and sales, using my communication method I use daily. I call it networking with a sales twist. I have tested the 5-Step Speed Networking Method among entrepreneurs, government workers, consultants, side hustlers, business owners, corporate employees, and sales people, who volunteered to be in my focus group. I figured out an easy method and it works!

Introduction

The top feedback from participants were:
- Increased confidence when starting a business conversation.
- Used precise words to limit rambling.
- Selling seemed easier with this method.

Speed networking provides a framework for all networking interactions. It also structures the conversation in concise presentations of what, why, value, and contact. This approach results in well-informed customers who perceive that you value their time and honor their attention.

Chapter One

Networking Is For You

IT'S NOT JUST FOR JOB SEEKERS

Speed Networking is for you—the entrepreneur, *sidepreneur*, also known as a person with a side hustle, small business owner, consultant, job seeker—who wants to utilize powerful and meaningful words to sell your products and services. People want to develop strong, meaningful connections and networks with other people. Life feels good when we are connected. I feel good as I write because I am connecting with you through this inspirational, informational book. Yet, when most of us think about networking, we usually only think of people who are searching for jobs at networking events. For years I networked only at happy hours or in designated places. For a long time, I had never thought of networking as a part of my daily routine. Have you?

Networking is usable in everyday situations, as well as at networking events. It is the exchange of information and energy between two or more people. It opens up a space for you to be seen, heard, and understood by your listeners as a valuable person sharing a heart-centered message about who you are, what you can give, how you give it, and why they need it. Ideally, you will be precise and descriptive in your words. You will have good and memorable energy exchanged between you and your potential customer. During this exchange, you should offer some type of usable knowledge, solve a problem, or sell your products or services.

This definition of networking will be the foundation for creating the five steps that encourage you to engage in short, yet meaningful, conversations to help you attract more friends, business opportunities, and customers.

Many entrepreneurs have told me they attended as many happy hours and networking events as they possibly can in hopes of meeting customers. Before attending any of those events, make sure to look at the event's format. If it is in a large club, serving alcohol, and featuring DJs, you might be going to a party disguised as a networking event. If held in a private room, with a microphone, hosted by a group leader, then most likely it will be a professional networking event. Magical moments happen during networking. The more you network, the more opportunities you have to grow your business.

WHAT'S THE DIFFERENCE?
Happy Hour versus Networking Event

My networking journey began because my friend and I share November birthdays. A mutual friend invited us to dinner. We decided to eat at a local night club/restaurant that had been struggling. During dinner, the entrepreneur owner and her chef came over to our table to talk and learn more about us. They asked us to invite more of our friends to their establishment. The owner asked us to host a night. I have often wondered why the owner asked us. The only reason that makes sense is because the owner must have known that we could influence our community to attend our events. After all, we are connected to other professional women in various industries. We decided to start a First Fridays Networking Happy Hour.

We got to work creating a buzz. We implemented a few strategies to get our community interested in participating. We networked face-to-face with our closest friends. We started a Twitter handle. We posted pictures and announcements on Facebook. We created a Facebook fan page. We invited people using texts and Evite invitations. We had business cards with a mission statement about networking. People came to our networking events. Business in the night club/restaurant began to boom again, particularly during our events. The First Fridays Networking Happy Hour event was to focus on networking. However, after years of observation, I realized very few attendees networked.

For two years, my business partners and I hosted a festive First Fridays Networking Happy Hour for professional women. We wanted to create a space for professional women to network and socialize. We thought we could give professional women a platform to financially support each other's businesses and creative projects in our beautiful city, the nation's capital. All of this happened through networking, collaborating, and bringing value to a night club/restaurant owner who was in need of more business in her venue. The club owner had told us she was dissatisfied with her clientele. She was not attracting the type of clientele she desired. Without a clear vision and road map for your business, you will always be on a detour.

We never lived up to the mission statement on our business card. Occasionally, I encouraged networking by inviting someone to take the microphone and announce the name of their business over loud music and roaring conversations. After awhile, the event transformed into a social party with loud, glaring rap music, cocktails, and hot finger foods. The attendees did not know how to network.

Dr. Maya Angelou said, "Do the best you can until you know better. Then, when you know better, do better."

Now I know better. Everything happens for a valid reason. The First Fridays Networking Happy Hour taught me a lot. Those Friday nights, surrounded by beautiful, professional women, were spectacular and so much fun. But, more importantly, it helped me to see my vision more clearly for the community of professional women who gathered monthly for two years. Although I did not fulfill the mission stated on the business card—to network—I learned some valuable lessons from that experience. After two years and two months, the attendance to the First Fridays Networking Happy Hour for professional women decreased and the nightclub/restaurant started to spiral downward. Soon after, the club was sold. With that news, our First Fridays abruptly ended.

WHAT IS YOUR CLEAR VISION FOR YOURSELF?

One of the best methods I can think of is sharing your vision through networking. Networking is a way to grow your business, build your brand, and support your community.

Books and networking events can help you find, as well as grow, your tribe.

There is a caterer in my city named Carlos. I first met Carlos' food at a party that my friend had for her daughter. I decided to network at the party and get to know as many people as possible. I was so impressed with the food I told everybody about Carlos' catering before I actually met Carlos. I hired him to cater several of my events and parties and referred him to many friends' businesses. He landed a $10,000 event and a standard annual catering contract with a non-profit organization based on networking with me. After ten years of referring him, the last time I spoke with Carlos, he was auditioning for *Shark Tank*.

Networking is powerful. We do it daily and many of us never measure the impact we are making. You are valuable. You are powerful. Your business can be like Carlos' business. Keep networking. The more you network, the better you become at connecting with others and ultimately increasing your sales.

So, you are saying to yourself, "I have a great business and provide an excellent service, but no one is promoting me." One question: How will you grow to your fullest capacity? When you effectively implement the 5-Step Speed Networking Method in this book, you should see a big difference in your return on the investment of time in yourself.

Chapter Two

The Basis For The 5-Step Speed Networking Method

> *"Don't' be afraid to give up the good to go for the great."*
> — John D. Rockefeller

Let us define speed networking by disassembling the two words that comprise the phrase. The word *speed* brings your attention to precise, concise, and awareness of timing in your words. *Networking* is the mechanism for value exchange between people, businesses, and brokers. Speed networking is a process for respecting the time resource in the exchange between you and the person with whom you are speaking.

DOUBLE MEANING OF SPEED NETWORKING

How many times have you attended a networking event or happy hour only to speak with one or two people in four hours? We are all guilty of it mostly because we are fearful of meeting and approaching new people. We find a comfort zone and we stay in it. With the 5-Step Speed Networking Method, you will see how the networking formula helps you move from person to person. In the speed networking events I host, a time clock limits interactions. I take the fear out of networking by structuring the event so everyone easily rotates around the room to meet each other in a timely manner, using the formula for the 5-Step Speed Networking Method.

Throughout this book, I will outline the details of how speed networking physically works. The 5-Step Speed Networking Method you will learn in this book will prepare you for various networking events. Like speed dating, there can be many different ways to do speed networking. The two settings that I teach, facilitate, and participate in work really well.

Rotation Setting requires all networking event attendees to sit at a long table, facing each other. The group leader encourages the attendees on the right side of the table to talk to the person facing them for a timed period of two minutes. After two minutes, the group leader says, "Switch speakers."

The Basis For The 5-Step Networking Method

The attendees on the left side of the table talk to the person facing them. After two minutes, the group leaders announce, "Rotate." The attendees on one side of the table rotate one seat over.

The goal of speed networking is to get everybody in the room to talk with each other. Breaks allow attendees to enjoy beverages and a quick bite of food. The group leader or the venue usually provides the food. A networking event is successful when you have made relevant connections that enhance your business growth.

Mic Setting requires a microphone and a stage. One attendee will speak on a mic to the entire audience for a two-minute period. After ten or so presentations, music offers an interlude by a DJ or music playlist from your smartphone. Sometimes, professional entertainers perform, if you have those types of people in your network. The audience is encouraged to take notes on speakers that interest them so individual networking and conversations can happen during the breaks. This method allows networkers to gain confidence speaking to large groups. Some group leaders allow question-and-answer sessions to take place after each entrepreneur presents.

A DEEPER LOOK AT NETWORKING
Take Inventory of Your Network

How can you increase your net worth through your networking? After all, as entrepreneurs, we want to generate revenue that sustains us throughout our lives. Studies show that we become the average of the five people with whom we spend most of our time.

Now is a good moment to take an awareness inventory of the daily activities performed by the top five people in your life.

1. What has each of them accomplished recently?

2. Are they operating at the levels you want to reach?

3. Are you being professionally uplifted or held down by networking with them?

4. What are they doing with your precious time invested in them?

Be honest with your observations, and true answers will surface in your mind. You will think twice about saying "Yes" to spending every weekend hanging out with your "What have you been up to lately?" friends, whose answer is always, "Oh nothing, just chillin." It may be time to start intentionally networking to open up your circle of influence.

The Basis For The 5-Step Networking Method

When I take time to build relationships with successful entrepreneurs, I am more likely to meet other people with similar mind-sets. When I am giving my time to activities that are enhancing my creativity, my education, my physical development, my earnings and my vision; I am very happy. I feel totally elevated, with high spirits and positive vibrational energy.

Time is a gift to the other person who is in your presence. What are you doing with your most valuable commodity? When you take time to speak with me, or vice-versa, we have shared a valuable resource of time. With the 5-Step Speed Networking Method, I will teach you how we can honor each other's gift of time.

Time is the most important element that can be leveraged when you are networking with others. Statistics show that people have a capacity to listen for only ten seconds. That is about ten words spoken out of your mouth. After that, your listener is likely having a beautiful daydreaming moment. Some of the listeners will naturally interrupt you just so they can stay alert. Speed networking and the 5-Step Speed Networking Method to creating short, yet meaningful, conversations will help you network effectively.

Speed networking is a skill to be practiced and made into a precise art form. Each of the steps will be introduced in a separate chapter. Your initial interaction will include the following five steps:

1. I AM.
2. What Do I Do?
3. Why I Do This.
4. Add Value.
5. My Contact Information.

INNOVATIVE NETWORKING WITH THE 5-STEP SPEED NETWORKING METHOD

You have so much you want to say, but the words in your mind won't come out of your mouth.

Your reach or penetration into the minds of others happens every time you speak. In my sales profession, every thirty seconds that I speak earns me thirty seconds more when I speak into the heart of my listener. Every thirty seconds that I speak, earns me thirty seconds more when I am resonating with my listener.

As a new entrepreneur, the value of your business must resonate with customers, suppliers, and other stakeholders.

The Basis For The 5-Step Networking Method

Another way to reiterate my message to you in the most comprehensive statement I can think of is as follows:

> When you are networking and selling, it is important that your words solve a problem, provide a solution, increase awareness as a speaker and a listener, gain knowledge about a specific subject, and/or receive an opportunity to experience an event, place, or thing from a perspective other than your own.

You might be able to transform your life and your business in a profound way because you allowed yourself to network with others.

Since you are living on planet earth, you are constantly networking, whether you are in your family's living room, or in the corporate boardroom. Almost every interaction with everyone is an open opportunity to network.

Take a moment right now and ask yourself a simple series of questions:

- When was the last time I networked with a new person face-to-face?

- What did I say?

- Was I rambling on and on?

- Did I repeat myself?

- How did I say it?

- Where was I?

- What were the results of my networking?

Like most people, you probably stated your name, your profession, and handed the listener a business card. The listener mirrored your behavior. Then, the two of you departed. Nothing gained. Nothing lost. You put the collected business card in the stack of business cards you already collected, and soon forgot why you have any of the business cards.

HOW CAN YOU RESHAPE NETWORKING?

You can reshape the way you interact and network. Your interactions will become more authentic, more powerful, and more useful. You are a powerful being, doing powerful things, in every moment of the day. You and your business can simply be different from everyone else, without trying. Different is memorable.

The Basis For The 5-Step Networking Method

As a uniquely created individual, you create unique things. No one in the world is identical to you. There are similar businesses, but none identical. Even franchises have variations. You can easily be different by just being yourself.

You are valuable. Every time you share your thoughts positively about an experience, you automatically set a prosperity cycle in motion for somebody. For example, when you gladly refer a friend to a delicious restaurant, a favorite movie, or a helpful website, you have created wealth for the person who created the restaurant, the movie, and the website. You have also given value to your friend who enjoys that restaurant, movie, or website. Good referrals never end. They are repeated. Remember, you are a powerful being, doing powerful things, in every moment of the day.

I want your numerous customers to set your prosperity cycle in motion as they refer your outstanding products and unforgettable services to many others. This prosperity cycle will start with *you*, by *you*, as *you* practice the innovative networking methods I have formulated. As Jim Rohn, entrepreneur, author, and speaker, once said, "Giving is better than receiving because giving starts the receiving process."

Chapter Three

Step 1—I AM

"The whole secret of a successful life is to find out what is one's destiny to do, and then do it."
— Henry Ford, founder, Ford Motor Company

I AM. This is a powerful statement. Whatever you state after saying "I AM" will make a lasting impression. It affirms how you exist on this planet. I AM are two powerful and creative words that define who you say you are. Even the tone, in which you say your full name, can be memorable or easily forgotten by your listener.

I AM can also indicate who you want to become in your business and in your career. Be bold and state who you want to be in your business, even if you are not quite there yet. Once you say it with conviction, you will become it through your inner belief.

Step 1—I AM

I AM should always be spoken with an authentic adjective that describes you. Before you can say with conviction and confidence who you really are, you have to know it for sure.

First, do you believe your own words, your own I AM statement? Have you heard anyone else tell you how he or she sees you? Have you heard people describing you as a brilliant marketer, a heart-centered person, a prolific writer, a creative thinker, an excellent problem solver, the best coach, an innovator, an abstract artist, or thought provoker?

Ask your friends, colleagues, mentors, and even family how they see you. Linger on the positive words you hear spoken about you. Tell them to repeat them. Repeat them yourself. Breathe in the positive words. Believe them. Start rehearsing your I AM statement aloud and often.

Proclaiming the energetic words of I AM will build an aura around you. The words will start living in your heart with clarity. I guarantee everyone will see your I AM before you say a word. When you introduce yourself, you will be amazingly confident and believable. Your words will flow from your mouth with power like your favorite song. The recipient will receive your words like a diamond ring during a marriage proposal. Yes! And, yes! Your listener will be intrigued and engaged in what you are sharing about who you say you are. Best of all, they will believe you.

The key elements needed to create your I AM statement are:

- Use an authentic adjective.
- Tell what you do and for whom.
- State what you created in one sentence.

Examples of I AM with an authentic adjective:

I am a *passionate* educator.

I am a *creative* business writer.

I am a *fun-loving* mother of twins.

I am a *dedicated* real estate agent.

I am an *abstract* artist.

I am an *experienced* contractor with the government.

I am a *successful* and *creative* entrepreneur.

I am an *empowering* business coach.

I am an *inspirational* and *transformational* speaker.

Step 1—I AM

CREATING YOUR "I AM"

Example 1:

Hello, my name is Cynthia Martin. I AM a heart-centered *(authentic adjective)* sales director and co-founder of a dental agency that coaches struggling dentists *(tell what you do for whom)* on how to practice integrative comprehensive dentistry *(state what you created in one sentence)* in order to increase their revenue.

Write out what you have in mind now:

Hello, my name is _____
_____.

I am a *(use an authentic adjective)* _____
_____

(tell what you do for whom) _____
_____
_____

(state what you created in one sentence).

Example 2:

Hello, my name is Cynthia Martin. I AM a dedicated *(authentic adjective)* coach for entrepreneurs who are having difficulty growing their businesses. I teach how to network and increase sales *(tell what you do for whom)*. I am the founder of an online resource called DC Speed Networking *(state what you created in one sentence)*.

Example 3:

Hello, my name is _____. I am a high-energy, fun-loving dance instructor! I will teach you how to move your hips, clap your hands, and make you forget you are working out! I created Dance Moves for Non-Dancers.

Now that you have some examples for Step 1, take some time to think about yourself and your business. On the following page, create your I AM.

Step 1—I AM

Write out what you have in mind now:

Hello, my name is _____.

I am a *(use an authentic adjective)* _____
_____

(tell what you do for whom) _____
_____
_____

(state what you created in one sentence).

Write it again:

Hello, my name is _____.

I am a *(use an authentic adjective)* _____
_____

(tell what you do for whom) _____
_____
_____

(state what you created in one sentence).

Try to write it once more. Each time you will become more concise with your words.

Hello, my name is _____
_____.

I am a *(use an authentic adjective)* _____
_____

(tell what you do for whom) _____
_____
_____

(state what you created in one sentence).

Great job!

Your goal is to meaningfully meet, not just causally greet, as many people as possible using this method. With this in mind, you do not want to add too many words to any of the steps. We have four more steps to go through, which will add layers of depth to the conversation.

One good habit to practice, when networking at an event, is to listen to as many conversations as possible. You will be able to get a general idea of most of the networkers in the room. This will increase your ability to become a valuable connector. Connectors are people who make introductions

Step 1—I AM

between networkers based on things learned during meaningful conversations.

Now that you have mastered Step 1, let's move on to the next step.

Chapter Four

Step 2—What Do I Do?

*"The most creative act you will ever undertake
is the act of creating yourself."*
—Deepak Chopra

Step 2 is very important. You will describe the action of your business using verbs and memorable adjectives. Simply state the transformation, change, or improvement you provide for the type of client who is looking for you, your products, or your services. It is your job to make sure your ideal clients know you exist. The only way for them to know is that you talk about yourself and what you can do for them.

In the pharmaceutical sales industry, we use visuals and pictures to show our listener what the products do. Most of

Step 2—What Do I Do?

us will retain information when pictures are associated with words. Better yet, messages related in a storytelling manner with pictures stain our minds even deeper. You will concisely describe what you do for your ideal clients and how you do it. This is your opportunity to sell with confidence and show with real pictures and/or mental descriptive pictures.

Your listeners need to hear how you can serve them, or someone they know, and meet their needs immediately. In other words, if you can solve problems for others, you can make a deal.

I challenge you, in this step, to create a small product literature piece. Here are three easy steps for creating a product literature piece or a sales page for your business.

1. Take photos of your products. If you don't have physical products, but you provide a service, create pages with your service descriptions. Use bullet points, be selective, and don't overcrowd the page.

2. Include a concise description page, a benefits page, and a transformation page that shows how your product or service solves problems and makes life better.

3. Use PowerPoint, Pages, or Keynote to build a short, eye-catching presentation to share.

4. Upload your presentation to your iPad, tablet or phone using an app that makes it simple to open your sales pages and talk to your listeners.

Hint: Please practice your presentation every day. You want to memorize it, flip back and forth between the pages with ease, prepare for objections and questions, and most impressively, sound conversational while you are sharing your presentation. You might not use your presentation at a networking event, but if you schedule a follow-up meeting, you will be prepared to shine.

If your product is not too bulky, show and demonstrate your actual product. Wear your company logo on a shirt. It is easy to print your logo from your computer onto photo paper and iron the logo onto a shirt. Make sure the company logo is over your heart so you will remember to speak from your heart. If you give away promotional items, make sure your logo is on them, or, at least, your mission statement.

EXPLORING TRANSFORMATION, CHANGE AND IMPROVEMENT

Transformation means you will teach your ideal clients how to expand their thinking. You will speak a sentence or two about how your service or product will move clients from

Step 2—What Do I Do?

where they are now to where they might aspire. Your words need to stretch their imagination. Your pictures or images will cement your words. When the mind grows, mental transformations happen. Like a domino effect, everything in its path transforms.

Change means movement, growth, or efficiency for your ideal client. When formulating a sentence about change, tell your clients how you can help them change from a current system that is, perhaps, time consuming to a newer system that saves time.

Improvement means personal benefit to your ideal client. Perhaps you are a business coach specializing in businesses that need more clients. Your sentence will explain how you help businesses retain more clients. If you are a dance instructor, your sentence will explain how you can help me reduce my waistline and get more physically fit. You might have knowledge about how to automate marketing funnel for emails. The main point here is that your sentence must inform the listener of how your products or services can help them accomplish a measurable goal.

Step 2 is What Do I Do? The key elements needed to create your What Do I Do? statement are as follows:

- Who is your ideal client?
- What service or product do I offer?

- What will the service or product do?
- What is the transformation, change, or improvement?

Example 1:

> I work with new dentists *(ideal clients)* to develop customized coaching programs *(service or product I have)* that will improve their clinical skills *(service will do)* and profoundly increase their annual incomes *(transformation, change, or improvement I provide)*.

Hint for selling with an object: My visual to cement my words and enhance my listener's experience with me might be an ink pen with the words written along the side of it: Sell More Dentistry, Save More Lives.

I would wait to give the ink pen to my listeners after I am finished talking. I want them to stay focused on my words.

Step 2—What Do I Do?

Your turn to write:

I work with _____
_____ *(your ideal client)* to _____
_____
(service or product you have) _____
_____ *(what it will do)*
_____*(the transformation, change, or improvement)*.

Example 2:

I work with new business owners *(ideal client)* to develop sales strategies *(service or product I have)* to teach new business owners how to sell their products *(what I do)* to their targeted and ideal customers. I also teach them how to track their sales growth *(improvement I provide)*.

Notice I used "new business owners" twice to make a point. You will need to do that so your ideal clients will hear you clearly.

Hint for selling a service business: Have a presentation on your iPad, tablet or phone. Also have the company logo in view of the listeners.

Write it once more. You get better with practice.

I work with _____
_____ *(your ideal client)* to _____
_____
(service or product you have) _____
_____ *(what it will do)*
_____*(the transformation, change, or improvement)*.

Example 3:

For people who don't wear shoes in their homes, and have aching feet *(who is your ideal client)*. I sell Footie Floaters *(what product I have)*, a cushioned sock, that will keep your feet comfortable *(what the product will do)* and your floors clean *(transformation, change, or improvement)*.

Hint for selling with a product: Footie Floaters are a physical product that I can show to my listeners. It is lightweight and fun to explore. In this case, put the product in the listener's hands while you are talking.

Step 2—What Do I Do?

Your turn to write:

I work with _____
_____ *(your ideal client)* to _____
_____
(service or product you have) _____
_____*(what it will do)*
_____*(the transformation,*
change, or improvement).

Write it once more. It gets better with lots of practice.

I work with _____
_____ *(your ideal client)* to _____
_____
(service or product you have) _____
_____*(what it will do)*
_____*(the transformation,*
change, or improvement).

As you practice Step 2: What Do I Do?, you will see how a few words can say a lot about you and how you do what you do. Take the time to craft your thoughts and grab the attention of the listener quickly. Your key words are the descriptions of your ideal clients and the problems and pains the ideal clients are experiencing. Describe the clients who will benefit most from your product or services as clear as possible.

Most of us who are listening will visualize someone who fits the description of your ideal client. As the listener who wants to be a resource during the speed networking experience, we can make an immediate referral or an introduction via text, like the referrals I made for Carlos the caterer. Ninety-nine percent of the time, your phone is already in your hands, just text the website to a friend who needs the product or service. The person you are networking with will appreciate your referral, and probably would type in the name of their website in your phone so you can easily save it to your phone. Better yet, take a picture of the product or make a mental note to follow-through later, if you do not have a minute to spare during the conversation.

Chapter Five

Step 3—Why I Do This

"The most powerful force on earth is the human soul on fire."
—Ferdinand Foch

In this step, I want you always to share your inner most passionate reason for your work. Listeners want to be helpful to you when they can feel your pure energy vibrating through your meaningful words.

What is your Why? The word "why" is part of the most commonly Googled Autocomplete feature in the world. "Why" usually brings out the authentic truth in us. The response to your stated "why" is usually well received, heard, and felt by your listener. Have you noticed a more favorable response from others after you have shared your authentic truth?

Why are you doing what you are doing right now? As reality shows have become extremely popular over the last decade, the best contestants are those with a "why" story attached to their reason for participating. The most successful pharmaceutical sales people I know have a big reason for getting out of bed every morning to sell the company's products. Most of us highly motivated sales representatives want to be at the top of the sales ranking, which usually leads to a big bonus payout and lots of peer-related recognition within the company. Most importantly, when you believe in what you are selling, products or services, you will be successful and helpful to others.

In everyday networking situations, we have a reason to talk about our "why." Think about why you told your best friend about a movie you liked. Think about why you patronize the same restaurant consistently. Think about why you are always willing to help others. The answers to the questions are because the movie resonated with you, the food is irresistible, and helping others makes you feel good. Every "why" has a field of energy around it. A vibration. A vision. An inspiration. A certain feeling that transforms your spirit. What is your "why?"

Step 3—Why I Do This

When you attend networking events, you might want to have a defined mission and vision for your life clearly thought out in your head. It sounds too deep for networking, but if you don't define who you are, what you want, and why you want it, you will become anything to anyone; you have to decide who you are. You will take on any jobs, work with people you don't like, and take any kind of pay. Trust me, you will not be happy for long.

A lesson learned is that when I clearly embraced my skills, defined my value, stated who I wanted to work with, and started talking and writing about all of it with conviction, I quickly attracted the companies, clients, and colleagues seeking out my qualities. Speak your reality into existence. Meet as many people as possible. Engage your friends in your dreams and your business needs. Ask for support. Get feedback on your ideas from people who you do not know, networking is a great place to do it. They will tell you the truth.

For example, if someone asks you, "Have you noticed the increase in trucks and white vans that have ladders on top of them as you are driving on the highways?" Your first answer is probably "No." But, now that the words have been spoken and a visual has been created for you, you now see several trucks and white vans with ladders on the top all day, every day. Pay attention. Imagine when you paint the indelible picture of who you are, how you purposefully transform lives, who you serve, and why you do it, all of this becomes real to the listener. Soon, people who need your products and services will keep appearing to the person and to you. It goes both ways. The subject will keep coming up in conversations throughout the day.

As a networker, it is your job to talk about whom you know, what you know, and make that lasting connection in the minds that you encounter each day. There are no coincidences. You are reading this book to learn how to bring unforgettable value to yourself and share lasting value with others.

> *"When you increase your value, you increase the value of others around you."*
> —Cynthia D. Martin

Because of the transparency in the world now with all of our personal information being readily shared on apps, privacy does not exist. Why not share your "why" when you have a warm, human, face-to-face, voice-to-voice moment during networking? Make your message of "why" very clear, and clients who can benefit from your "why" will come to you.

Step 3—Why I Do This

All successful movements in history have a strong "why" described by its passionate leaders exuding powerful energy. You can do the same when you are talking about your business, when you are talking about why you want that new job, and when you are selling your new ideas during a meeting. You can do it when you are selling your products, and even when you are referring others to things that transformed, changed, or improved your life.

As an entrepreneur, why are you doing your business? What motivates you to build your business consistently? When you come up with your answer, you will feel the energetic excitement in your heart. You will be ready to talk to anybody who will listen. It is a great feeling!

What is your mission and your vision? Write it down and live it. If you can't live it, you have written down the wrong words. Try again. You can share your product, passion, or service with every interaction you have during your networking experience or any personal or media interaction. You can do it!

If you are seeking a job or contract work, you will need to know your "why," too. There was one question asked most of me during job interviews: "Why do you want to change from your current job?" My answer always centered on my mission and my vision for my life. When my "why" matched the company's "why," we made a deal. We were each other's ideal client. When my "why" did not match, we moved on. However, I did tell and email industry peers to see if they wanted to explore the job opportunity that was not right for me.

As you practice Step 3: Why I Do This, remember to evoke lasting feelings for your listeners through your spoken words.

The key elements needed to create your "Why" statement are the following:

- State your mission or your vision.

- State a passionate reason for your work.

- Use words that paint a picture in the listener's mind.

Example 1:

> I believe that dental health determines your overall health. Poor dental health can shorten your lifespan (*my vision, my mission*). An untapped, uneducated market exists in dentistry (*passionate reason for my work*). I am educating patients and creating ways to empower dentists to do better dental work. We use dental images to educate patients and to teach dentists (*paint a picture in the mind*).

Step 3—Why I Do This

Write about your *Why*:

I believe that_____
_____
_____ *(your mission)*.
I intend to _____
_____
_____*(passionate reason for your work)*.
It is like _____
_____
_____*(use words that paint a picture)*.

Example 2:

My *(mission)* is to teach new business owners to define and reach their growth goals. My business success happens because many people help me. I will help you *(passionate reason for work)*. With me, it's business boot camp. I am relentless, loud, and unremitting. You will grow your business *(energetic words paint a picture)* when you work with me.

Example 3:

I'm committed to bring comfort to you *(mission, vision)* and making you feel extraordinary when you use my products *(passionate reason for your work)*. When you wear Footie Floaters on your tired feet, every step feels like you're walking on fluffy clouds *(words that paint a picture)*.

Write about your *Why*:

I believe that_____
_____
_____ *(your mission)*.
I intend to _____
_____
_____*(passionate reason for your work)*.
It is like _____
_____
_____*(use words that paint a picture)*.

Step 3—Why I Do This

Write it once more.

Write about your *Why*:

I believe that_____

_____

_____ *(your mission).*

I intend to _____

_____

_____*(passionate reason for your work).*

It is like _____

_____

_____*(use words that paint a picture).*

Congratulations! You are smart and determined because Steps 1, 2, and 3 are not easy to do until you spend time thinking deeply and profoundly about yourself. Do you realize how much time you spend forming opinions about others and what they are doing or not doing? I've taken part in conversations about celebrities—their lives and what they do. Have you ever observed how passionate people talk about celebrities? My inner thoughts are always: *I wish this person would talk about themselves with conviction and passion. I'd love to get to know them.* I've even wished I could talk about myself with conviction and passion and someone would actually listen.

I'm so glad you have spent that time thinking about yourself. Keep that self-momentum in motion. You have worked diligently. I am proud of you! Now it is time to start talking about yourself to people you meet. Just remember that good communication is mimicked. Notice that when you are communicating with someone and you are in alignment with your thoughts, your body language will mirror each other. If your hands are in your pant pockets, the person you are talking to will put their hands in their pockets. If you sit down and cross your legs, the person you are in conversation with will cross their legs. Once they mimic you, you know you have connected.

Even though the person you are speaking to may not know the 5-Step Speed Networking Method you are using and implementing, they will try to reflect your communication style. Without consciously knowing it, the both of you are learning from each other in a meaningful engagement. The prosperity cycle is in motion.

BEYOND THE THIRTY-SECOND PITCH

By now, we have a networking conversation, not a traditional thirty-second pitch. You are compiling a real quick conversation that you can use as a pitch in many ways. What

Step 3—Why I Do This

is a pitch, according to me? Well, do you know about the term "sales pitch?" The term refers to a presentation usually lasting thirty to forty-five seconds. However, my definition of pitch expands to include the 5-Step Speed Networking Method. This expansion creates short, yet meaningful, conversations for networking. So far, you have created Step 1: I AM, Step 2: What Do I Do?, and Step 3: Why I Do This. These five steps are more in-depth and take longer to execute than a traditional pitch. However, let us take a moment to talk about the pitch. The definition of *pitch,* as it relates to networking and selling, I have expanded it. You are on your way to creating a comprehensive pitch, which means you have all the elements of your business wrapped in one extended statement.

Your pitch includes sounds or words that have a frequency that are clear and precise enough to be distinguished from other people's words or different from others who are doing things similar to you. Your pitch is like music. It has a frequency that resonates with the listener or not. When it resonates, you connect and sell.

Once you complete the 5-Step Speed Networking Method, you can use your creation in the following ways:

- Your extended personal pitch

- Your business pitch

- Your sales pitch
- Your introduction pitch
- Your resume pitch
- Your written contract language
- Your headlines on your media accounts

I might not have listed all the creative ways here, but the time you are spending developing the five steps for networking will bring enormous value to your life in everyday situations as well. Implementation and execution are the key factors. The more you talk about your ideas, your business, and your abilities, the more they become real to others and reachable within yourself.

Chapter Six

Step 4—Add Value

*"Success is...knowing your purpose in life,
growing to reach your maximum potential,
and sowing seeds that benefit others."*
—John C. Maxwell

What is value? It is giving of yourself, your services, your products, sharing your opinions and knowledge and making a referral. There is a litany of ways to add value to your listener. Usually, value is something that can be implemented immediately by the listener and they can see results if they follow-through. The value you give should solve a problem, big or small, that your listener is having. Today's marketing rule is first give usable value over and over, and then ask for the sale.

My theory is to share your most favorite things because you will be able to talk about them with ease. The passion side of your personality will illuminate and you will speak with a smile. Your goals are to open the minds of the people you encounter face-to-face, the ones who read your emails, and your followers on social media. I feel very good when I have learned new information. I feel accomplished when I have shared usable value with others.

Offer something that will enhance a life. Examples include articles from online magazines, statistics, website links, apps, free eBooks, podcasts, Twitter handles, personal introductions, free samples of your products or services, venues to visit, YouTube videos, recommend seminars, social media personalities to follow, sales tips, free webinars you have completed, and so much more.

As you develop Step 4, think about the value you can add to your listener. The key elements needed to create your "Add Value" statement are the following:

- What value do I give?

- Give a website, app, free offer, or something to share.

- Make an introduction to someone or something new for your listener.

- Make a referral for a potential client to your listener, if possible.

Step 4—Add Value

Example 1:

I have been in sales for seventeen years. If you want sales tips for your business *(what value you can give)*, I can help you. Go to my website, I have daily tips *(website)*, or follow @Inc. Magazine on Twitter *(make an introduction that is new to the listener)*. There are great articles I read daily. What sales methods do you currently use (intro to sell books)?

Write your thoughts here.

I _____
_____*(what value you give)*. ___

_____
_____*(website, app, free something to share)*. _____
(make an introduction). _____
_____ *(make a referral)*.

Example 2:

If you want to learn more about your dental health, follow us @TeachMeDental *(what value you give)* and you will see a wealth of information about your teeth. Visit my website DrGlasper.com *(website)*. If you or your family wants a free dental evaluation, I can get you one with Dr. Glasper *(free service and an introduction)*.

Example 3:

I have a fun website with a section about caring for your tired feet *(value you give)*. When you visit my website *(website)*, you can get some deep discounts on my Footie Floaters, too *(offer something to share)*.

It is your turn to write your Step 4. Write your thoughts here.

I _____

_____*(what value you give)*. ___

_____

_____*(website, app, free something to share)*. _____

Step 4—Add Value

*(make an introduction). _____
_____ (make a referral).*

Write it once more. Be more concise.

*I _____
_____(what value you give). ___
_____
_____(website, app, free something to share). _____
(make an introduction). _____
_____ (make a referral).*

Write it again. I know, it sounds great.

*I _____
_____(what value you give). ___
_____
_____(website, app, free something to share). _____
(make an introduction). _____
_____ (make a referral).*

Sometimes, your information and the value you share may not be related to your product. It might be something that will deepen your rapport with whom you are networking.

If you happen to go off topic, try to relate whatever you are talking about back to your business, product, or service. You always want to end your conversation about your business and about you. After all, your goal is to carve out space in the person's mind for you and your business, even when you are not present.

Chapter Seven

Step 5—My Contact Information

Traditionally, paper business cards have been the way to share contact information and end a networking moment. If you are still using paper business cards, make sure you have all your social media connections and, most importantly, a phone number for credibility. People feel more secure about doing business with you if you are reachable by phone, even if they never call you.

Let us innovate the way you share your contact information by ending the networking moment digitally. I created a digital business card I can text, using Canva.com.

Steps for making digital business cards using Canva.com

1. Go to Canva.com and set up an account

2. Sign in using your email and password

3. Left side of the screen, click on Your Designs, click [+] within Create A Design

4. Scroll down to Marketing Materials and click on Business Card

5. See options for designs on the left side of the screen, choose a free one

    a. Choose one that fits your business and the space you need to add your information

6. Edit card with your information

    a. Change text by clicking in the text box. Modify with relevant information.

    b. Click on name and delete, add your name, tag line, phone numbers, or website, twitter, or whatever you need

    c. Change the font type, size and color by highlighting text box

    d. Change font effects by selecting [] down arrow

7. Save changes by clicking on <File> on the top-left side of the screen

Step 5—My Contact Information

    a. You may save after each change

8. Share your business card by clicking on <Share> on the top-right side of the screen

    a. Fill in and email address and send to friends for review

    b. You may also share by using Facebook or Twitter

9. Download your business card by clicking on <Download> on the top-right side of the screen

    a. Select the type of file you would like to down load (.jpg/.png/.pdf)

10. Congratulations! You are ready to promote your business!

Simply reference the instructions on how to create a digital business card you can text and be amongst the first to offer a digital business card. I like to text my business card so my listener can save my information under their contact information, which can be done within seconds of the exchange. Ask the listener if you can text your business card. Once the texted business card is saved, it automatically creates a contact in the phone. Making a digital introduction, from

Step 4, to potential clients is simple as forwarding a text with the business card embedded in it. Another way to add value to the conversation, the person receiving your texted business card will want to know how you did it. This is an opportunity to set up a time to teach them. You see how you are adding more value to that person's life by helping them create their digital business card.

Another thing to do is to ask if you can add your listener to your email list so you can maintain a deep connection. Building your email list is important because you can educate your readers and sell your readers at the same time.

The key elements needed to create your "Share My Contact Information" statement are the following:

- Express your gratitude about the interaction.

- Ask for permission to connect.

- Follow-up on promises, if necessary.

Example 1:

> I really enjoyed talking with you about our businesses and ways we can help each other *(express gratitude about the interaction)*. Let's stay connected. I would like to text my business card to you *(permission to connect)*. What is your phone number? Thank you.

Step 5—My Contact Information

Hint: You have just captured the listener's phone number. Now you can create a contact in your phone. Make sure you text a 'nice to have met you' text. Also, the receiver of the business card text can forward the texted business card to potential clients to help spread the word about your business. This action kicks off the cycle of prosperity for you.

Write your thoughts now.

> I really enjoyed meeting you and discussing _____ *(express your gratitude about the interaction)*. I would like to stay connected. Can I text my business card to you *(ask for permission to connect)*? I will be in touch soon *(follow-up on promise)*.

Example 2:

> I really enjoyed meeting you and getting to know about you and your business *(express your gratitude about the interaction)*. May we stay connected *(ask for permission to connect)*? I will connect you to people who need you. Add my contact information to your phone. I can text my business card to you right now. What is your phone number? I will text you to

set up a meeting to continue our conversations *(follow-up on promise)*.

Hint: When you send a follow-up text for a meeting request, always include three meeting options with dates, times, and locations. Ask the receiver to choose one. It is your responsibility to confirm the date and time for the meeting.

Hint: Send a meeting reminder one day before the meeting, and be prepared to continue the short and meaningful conversation.

Write it once more.

> I really enjoyed meeting you and discussing _____ *(express your gratitude about the interaction)*. I would like to stay connected. Can I text my business card to you *(ask for permission to connect)*? I will be in touch soon *(follow-up on promise)*.

Write your Step 5 again. It gets easier.

> I really enjoyed meeting you and discussing _____ *(express your gratitude about the interaction)*. I would like to stay connected. Can I text my business card to

Step 5—My Contact Information

you *(ask for permission to connect)*? I will be in touch soon *(follow-up on promise)*.

> "There is no such thing as a good idea unless it is developed and utilized."
> —Kekich Credo

Congratulations! You have completed the 5-Step Speed Networking Method to creating short, yet meaningful, conversations for networking. You now have a nice working guideline for your next networking event. Remember the five steps can work in many different environments. You can utilize your words when you are connecting with people in your everyday situations and conversations. The next time your friends or family members ask, "What have you been up to?" you can reply by using some of the five steps you created. Once you get comfortable talking through your five Steps, you can use them out of order, and easily use them to answer questions about your business.

Keep a copy of your 5-Step Speed Networking Method script in your pocket to boost your confidence as you network. Better yet, keep it on your smartphone to refer to when you are networking. Keep the five steps handy for when you are attending meetings with people who might need your services or products.

Chapter Eight

The Finished Product

THE SCRIPT IN ONE CONTINUOUS NARRATIVE

The finished product will flow like this:

Hello, my name is Cynthia Martin. "I AM" a dedicated coach and seminar facilitator for new entrepreneurs who are having difficulty growing their businesses. I teach how to speed network to increase sales. I am the founder of an online resource called DC Speed Networking.com.

I work with new business owners and entrepreneurs to develop speed networking

Step 5—My Contact Information

strategies using my 5-Step Speed Networking Method formula that will help to sell their products to their targeted and ideal customers. I also teach them how to develop sales visuals to make their words more impactful and memorable.

My mission is to teach new business owners and entrepreneurs to define and reach their growth goals. My business success happens because others help me. I will help you. With me, it's business boot camp. I am relentless, realistic, and unremitting. You will grow your business when you work with me.

I've been in sales for seventeen years. If you want sales tips for your business, I can give you thirty minutes of help. Go to my website: www.dcspeednetworking.com to learn more about speed networking, text, or follow @DCSpeednetwork and @IAmCyMartin on social media.

I like meeting motivated people like you. May I text you my business card? Save it in your phone contacts. Feel free to forward it to others. May I add you to my email list? I will invite you to a speed networking event.

YOUR WORDS ARE YOUR WAY

Now that you have your words written out in the most concise way possible and have practiced your networking language, you are ready to attend a speed networking event. I am sure you will be the most prepared person in the room.

Your words are your entryway into meaningful conversations that convert into follow-ups that lead to sales. The more people you impact with your meaningful words, the more your business will prosper. Your potential to attract more customers through referrals will most likely increase as well. The key to getting the most leverage from using the 5-Step Speed Networking Method is your follow-through and follow-up with each of the meaningful conversations you have with people you meet. In business building and in sales, nothing happens until the follow-up happens.

Remember, in life you only get what you give, and the only thing that is missing in a business relationship is what you are not giving. During my seventeen-year sales career, my sales have soared and grown exponentially when I was consistent with my customers. I've also experienced dips and declines in my sales when I was not focused on my customer's needs. So, if you give lots of referrals, which starts the cycle of prosperity for all involved, connect people to each other, support small businesses, be of service to those who need you, it will all come back to you in powerful ways as you continue to build your business.

The Finished Product

Networking can be fun and effective when you prepare for the opportunity. I hope you will use the 5-Step Speed Networking Method to create short and meaningful conversations to build your business, not just for networking, but also in everyday situations.

Powerful words sell products and services.

ACKNOWLEDGEMENTS

A sincere thank you to all the wonderfully interesting entrepreneurs, side hustlers, and corporate friends who are participating in the DC Speed Networking events in the Washington, DC metropolitan area. I am forever grateful for your feedback, support, and encouragement.

A special thank you to Joy Zarembka for her editing skills.

Most importantly, thank you to my focus group and network of dedicated friends who come when I call.

Maria Queen - Abstract Artist
Marva Street – Art Curator
Vicky More – Digital Designer
Wallene Garrett – Analyst
Tonya Hayes – CEO, Efficient Transport LLC
Lori Jennings – Broadcast TV Director
Toysha Walker – Business Consultant
Yumika Hughes – Medical Sales Consultant
Andrea Wooten – Life Insurance Agent
Afton Walters – Admissions Counselor
Lanada Williams – Psychotherapist

Together, we create rich experiences and memorable moments.

For questions and comments, please contact me.
Cynthia@DCSpeedNetworking.com

Visit me online at DCSpeedNetworking.com

Network with me on Twitter:
@DCspeednetwork
@IAmCyMartin

Connect with me on Facebook:
DCSpeedNetworking

Speed Networking

Five Simple Steps to Sell Your Products and Services

WORKBOOK

Table of Contents

Introduction 75

Instructions 77

A Look at Mindset 78

Mindset Exercise 80

Getting Started 83

Step 1— I AM 85

Step 2—What Do I Do? 93

Step 3—Why I Do This 99

Step 4—Add Value 104

Step 5—My Contact Information 109

Introduction

This workbook is for entrepreneurs and people with side hustles who want to learn how to speed network. I strongly recommend you read the entire book before attempting to complete the workbook so you will see the benefits of networking more clearly. The concepts discussed in the book support the importance of the 5-Step Speed Networking Method, which is the foundation for building your networking dialogue.

This workbook will assist you in creating your meaningful, concise networking dialogue that thoroughly describes who you are and precisely defines your products or your services. Each section is a step-by-step guide that allows you to choose words to fill in the blanks. You will also have blank areas to use to brainstorm your thoughts.

Some sections have examples or suggestions. The examples are meant to stimulate your mind and jump start you to thinking about how you want to present yourself and your business so you can start your cycle of prosperity.

The next time you are standing in the grocery store line, or getting a shared ride, you can easily start a conversation using any of the steps in The 5-Step Speed Networking Method.

Instructions

Your challenge is to complete The 5-Step Speed Networking Method. Your goal is to create a networking dialogue you can use immediately. Your mission is to talk about your products or your services every day to at least one person per day.

If your words are memorable and you are dynamic, that one person will tell someone about your products or services. Imagine reaching sixty folks a month in just two minutes of human interaction. You can do it. Your return on the investment of your time will most likely lead to incremental, monthly increases in your revenue.

> *"Before you can make a connection with someone else, you will need to make a deep connection with yourself."*
>
> —Cynthia D. Martin

A Look at Mindset

In psychologist Carol Dweck's book, *Mindset: The New Psychology of Success*, she defines mindset as a self-perception or self-theory people think about themselves. Dr. Dweck explains two mindsets. Fixed mindset—a limited self-perception and Growth mindset—an unlimited self-perception.

Let's take a look at mindset as it relates to networking and connecting with people. From my perspective, there are two types of mindset when it comes to networking: Comfort Zone mindset and Forward Thinking mindset.

Comfort Zone mindset is displayed by the person who shake hands, exchange business cards and quickly ends the interaction. The Comfort Zone mindset person will not ask meaningful questions. The individual is very polite but hesitant to connect with others unless an immediate benefit is foreseeable.

The Forward Thinking mindset is displayed by a person who networks with everyone, ask probing questions, and adds value to the conversation. This person is open to exploring possibilities. The good news is that if you see yourself with a Comfort Zone mindset, you can develop a Forward Thinking mindset with a little practice.

How does mindset manifest itself?

Mindset is determined by your innate or inherit thoughts and by the people or culture who influence your thoughts. Your mindset is expressed through your mentality (disposition, attitude, mood), which is defined as your way of thinking. Your mentality shows up or can be seen in your communication and in your perpetual habits. However, your mindset can shift and change based on situations, goals, and people who influence you.

Mindset Exercise

Two important questions for you to ponder before you start The 5-Step Speed Networking Method are: What is your mindset? Who are the five folks you spend the most time with? Look at their mindsets, and you will begin to see yours. Most likely, the six of you share similar mindsets.

What do you admire about the people you spend the most time with? _____
_____
_____
_____
_____
_____
_____
_____

What areas do you wish they would grow? _____
_____
_____
_____
_____
_____
_____
_____
_____
_____

Workbook: A Look at Mindset

The right mindset can help you leverage and achieve the simplest tasks to the most complex accomplishments.

Take a moment to reflect on your mindset. Check the words that reflect your mindset today, not necessarily where you want to be. Be truthful with yourself.

Comfort Zone Mindset	Forward Thinking Mindset
☐ No real effort	☐ Achiever
☐ Blames others	☐ Learner
☐ Insecure	☐ Strategic
☐ Fearful	☐ Game changer or catalyst for change
☐ Procrastinator	
☐ Need validation	☐ Confident
☐ Playing it safe	☐ Choosing happiness
☐ Regret	☐ Trusting relationships
☐ Hiding your talents	☐ Embracing the unknown
☐ Surviving	☐ Determination
☐ Dull life	☐ Entrepreneurial
☐ Negative thinking	☐ Creative
☐ Denying your dreams	☐ Optimistic
☐ Self-doubting	☐ Seeking your dreams
☐ False superiority	☐ Global
☐ Complacent	☐ Ideological
☐ Critical	☐ Emotional resilience
☐ Feels stuck	☐ Persistent
	☐ Collaborative
Total _____	Total _____

Now that you are aware of your mindset, do you have a Comfort Zone mindset or Forward Thinking mindset? The higher total represents who you are right now. Your thoughts might reflect a little of both. The answer does not matter at this moment. We will revisit the mindset exercise after you have implemented your lessons in the workbook.

Getting Started

Speed networking is a skill to be practiced and made into a precise art form. Each of the steps will be introduced in a separate section of this workbook.

Each of the five sections has questions or statements that you will ponder and then answer as it relates to your products or services. Use your well thought out answers to fill in the blanks in each section.

I have provided suggestions, in the form of examples, to help stimulate your thinking about yourself. If the suggestions are applicable to you, use the examples to build your speed networking dialogue. Circle the suggestions as you go along. Use the suggestions to fill in the appropriate blanks. At the end of the five-step process, your goal will be met, but only if you do all of the exercises.

With a little effort, you will have a speed networking dialogue you can use immediately to grow your business.

Your initial interaction will include the following five steps:

1. I AM
2. What Do I Do?
3. Why I Do This
4. Add Value
5. My Contact Information

Step 1—I AM

I AM should always be spoken with an authentic adjective that describes you. Before you can say with conviction and confidence who you really are, you have to know it for sure. I AM can also indicate who you want to become in your business and in your career. Be bold. Be fearless. Own your authenticity.

To create your I AM statement, the key elements needed are:
- Use an authentic adjective.
- Tell what you do and for whom.
- State what you created in one sentence.

Each of the key elements will be explained below. I have provided examples to assist you in exploring and completing each of the key elements. Here are several examples. Circle the one that applies to you and then write your choice in the space provided.

- Chose an authentic adjective or create your own.

  I am a *passionate* educator.
  I am a *creative* business writer.
  I am a *fun-loving* mother of twins.
  I am a *dedicated* real estate agent.

I am an *abstract* artist.
I am an *experienced* contractor with the government.
I am a *successful* and *creative* entrepreneur.
I am an *empowering* business coach.
I am an *inspirational* and *transformational* speaker.

Here are more authentic adjectives to assist you in thinking about you and your business:

- Expert
- Conservative
- Motivational
- Systematic
- Compassionate
- Empathetic
- User-friendly
- Powerful
- Top-ranked
- Loving
- Determined
- Robust
- Interactive
- Truth-seeker
- Thorough
- Peaceful
- Introspective
- Unbiased
- Maximizer
- Regulated
- Heart-centered
- Ethical
- Active
- Bodacious
- Developing
- Aspiring
- Established
- Eloquent
- Intentional
- Purposeful
- Beautiful
- Reassuring
- Reliable
- Connector
- Uplifting
- Adaptable
- Service oriented
- Cheerful
- Aligned
- Optimistic
- Dependable
- Friendly
- Harmonious
- Understanding
- Strategic
- Achiever
- Analytical
- Insightful
- Cultivating
- Cost-effective
- Facilitative
- Fearless
- Trustworthy
- Competitive
- Restorative
- Unshakable
- Intellectual
- Original
- Five-star
- Attentive

Workbook: Step I—I AM

- By-the-book
- Considerate
- Committed
- Practical
- Goal-oriented
- Efficient
- Cutting-edge
- Engaged
- Thriving
- Decisive
- Investigative
- Inclusive
- Methodical
- Inspiring
- Easy to reach
- Money-making
- Enthusiastic
- Diligent
- Eco-friendly
- Visionary
- Meaningful
- Supportive
- Magnetic
- Emerging
- Transformative

List other adjectives that describe you:

_____
_____
_____
_____
_____
_____
_____
_____
_____
_____
_____
_____
_____
_____

Speed Networking

Write out what you have in mind now:

Hello, my name is_____
I am a *(use an authentic adjective)* _____
_____.

Now it's time to think about what you do and for whom. This means you will use a few words to precisely describe the main action that you do in your business on a daily basis. What action generates income and who are you doing the action for?

- **Tell what you do and for whom.**

Here are some suggestions and examples. These will likely not describe you, but put a check beside those that speak to you.

- ☐ Coaches struggling entrepreneurs
- ☐ Teaches artistic children's photography
- ☐ Strategist for branding new products
- ☐ Guides hikes for communities
- ☐ Paints family portraits
- ☐ Organizes closets for busy moms
- ☐ Edits books for self-publishing authors

Workbook: Step I—I AM

- ☐ Sells life insurance to middle-aged professionals
- ☐ Photographs newborn babies
- ☐ Develops apps for businesses
- ☐ Publicist for large corporations
- ☐ Virtually assists busy mothers
- ☐ Teaches gardening skills
- ☐ Caters events
- ☐ Event planner for children's parties
- ☐ Design logos
- ☐ Motivates women to lose weight
- ☐ Transforms men into fashion consciousness
- ☐ Performs for school-aged audiences
- ☐ Tutors teens with learning disabilities
- ☐ Markets products for distributors
- ☐ Sells jewelry online for women and girls
- ☐ Fitness instructor for overweight people
- ☐ Writes resumes for specific industries
- ☐ Motivational speaker who trains the trainer

- ☐ Accountant for start-ups
- ☐ Handy person for homeowners

Review those you liked and jot down your specific service or business and for whom.

Write yours here:

*(tell what you do for whom)*_____
_____
_____
_____.

- **State what you created in one sentence.**

You will state the purpose of your business, product or service in one sentence. The name of your business may not be important at this moment unless it explicitly paints a picture of what you do.

Keep it simple. You will have time to tell more about your business as you develop the other 5-Step Speed Networking Method. Here are just a few examples and suggestions. This area is very specific to your individual business.

- ◊ Creator of online resource called DC Speed Networking.com.
- ◊ The name of my business is Kids Parties Made Easy (this name tells the exact purpose of the business).

Workbook: Step I—I AM

- ◊ I created Dance Moves for Non-Dancers.
- ◊ Co-founder of a dental coaching agency.
- ◊ I developed an easy way to _____.
- ◊ I earn income, and so can you, by selling items online.
- ◊ My company teaches sales strategies.
- ◊ I provide year-round landscaping.
- ◊ I am a sleep coach for first-time moms with newborns who don't routinely sleep.
- ◊ I cook and deliver prepared lunches to summer camp programs for children.

Brainstorm your thoughts. Write the purpose of your business? Then choose only one sentence that captures your business.

Speed Networking

Write what you have created here:

_____
_____
_____ *(state what you created in one sentence).*

Write your completed thoughts here.

Hello, my name is_____
_____I am a *(use an authentic adjective)* _____
_____ *(tell what you do for whom)* _____
_____
(state what you created in one sentence).

Keep your momentum. One step is done.

Now that you have completed each of the key elements of Step 1—I AM, you can advance to the next step.

Step 2—What Do I Do?

Step 2 is very important. You will describe the action of your business or side hustle using verbs and memorable adjectives. Simply state the transformation, change, or improvement you provide for the type of client who is looking for you, your products, or your services. It is your job to make sure your ideal clients know you exist. The only way for them to know is by talking about yourself and what you can do for them.

You will need to be very clear about whom you want to serve in your business. What type of people do you want to design products and services for? "Everybody can benefit from my business" is the wrong answer. You have my permission to be narrow-minded and discriminatory.

Take a moment to define your ideal client. This helps your words resonate with the listeners who will benefit from networking with you. Build your foundation here.

- Start thinking about your ideal client.
- Is your ideal client any of the following?
- Small business owner
- Mother, child, father

- Side hustler
- Full-time entrepreneur
- Single professional
- Corporate employee
- Corporation
- Retiree
- Health care professional
- Gender: male or female, or both
- Age range that would most likely benefit from networking with you

- **What are you offering to your ideal client?**

- Inspiration/motivation like mindfulness meditation, goal setting
- Teach/learn a new skill like coding, sales strategies, networking
- "Done for you" service like building a website, or editing, graphic design
- Transformation to something significant like weight loss, body sculpturing

Workbook: Step 2—What Do I Do?

The key elements needed to create your What Do I Do? statement are as follows:

• Who is your ideal client?

Your ideal client will know they need to buy from you based on how you describe her or him. The ideal client will quickly self identify based on the words you speak. The words will resonate with that individual.

Look back at what you have already created in Step 1—I AM. You can expand your 'for whom' section and other sections you have already completed.

Examples and suggestions for: Who is your ideal client?

- ◊ Recent graduates, example, dentists who are seeking a job
- ◊ Women business owners who earn less than $50,000 a year and want to increase their revenue
- ◊ Young children ages seven to twelve years old who want to learn coding
- ◊ Struggling and experienced photographers looking for clients
- ◊ Elderly men who own homes and need a handy person

- ◊ Single mothers who are professionals and need chores done weekly
- ◊ People who want to blog, but don't know how
- ◊ Side hustlers starting a business and need guidance
- ◊ First time book authors who need an editor
- ◊ Entrepreneurs who want to buy Twitter ads
- ◊ Women who wear inexpensive costume jewelry, but looking for better quality
- ◊ Men who want life coaching after a divorce
- ◊ Side hustlers who want to learn selling skills and strategies

Write your ideal client description here:

I work with _____
_____ *(your ideal client)*.

- **What service or product do I offer? What will the service or product do? What is the transformation, change, or improvement?**

You can combine these three questions to formulate one concise sentence.

Workbook: Step 2—What Do I Do?

Briefly describe your product or service you offer to your ideal client. In that description, you will naturally tell what the service or product will do for the end user. It will just flow. You can do this in one to two sentences, at the most. The shorter the better. Don't glorify. Simplify.

The transformation, change, or improvement is based on who you identified as your ideal client and the problems those clients are having. You will provide a solution to the client's problems when they purchase your products or services.

Here are some examples and suggestions to guide you to keeping it simple. Design your sentence similar to the examples.

- ◊ I develop customized coaching programs that will improve dentists clinical skills and profoundly increase their annual incomes.

- ◊ I develop sales strategies to teach new business owners how to sell their products to their targeted and ideal customers.

- ◊ For people who don't wear shoes in their homes, and have aching feet, I sell Footie Floaters, a cushioned sock that will keep your feet comfortable and your floors clean.

- ◊ Through online courses, I teach product entrepreneurs how to purchase Twitter ads that target their ideal clients. My online courses will increase Twitter followers for product entrepreneurs and create an audience who may buy their products.

Write yours here:

I work with _____ _____ *(your ideal client)* to _____ _____
(service or product you have) _____ _____ *(what it will do)* _____*(the transformation, change, or improvement)*.

Step 3 — Why I Do This

In this step, I want you always to share your inner most passionate reason for your work. Listeners want to be helpful to you when they can feel your pure energy vibrating through your meaningful words.

Remember to evoke lasting feelings for your listeners through your spoken words in the "Why I Do This" section.

The following are the key elements needed to create your "Why" statement:

- **State your mission or your vision.**
- **State a passionate reason for your work.**
- **Use words that paint a picture in the listener's mind.**

Each of the key elements will be explained. I have provided examples to assist you with exploring and completing each of the key elements.

- **State your mission or your vision**

Is there a written mission for your business or side hustle you incorporate into your daily operations? Do you have a long-term vision for your business or side hustle that you work to achieve daily?

You can start by expressing a strong belief, a burning inner desire, or your passion that you have converted to a profit. Create your mission or your vision similar to the following:

- ◊ I believe dental health determines your overall health. Poor dental health can shorten your life span.

- ◊ I believe networking is the first step in starting the cycle of prosperity that ignites the sales cycle.

Write your mission and your vision using powerful words that exactly capture your belief.

Workbook: Step 3—Why I Do This

- **Now write your mission or your vision.**

    Write about your *Why*:

    I believe that_____
    _____
    _____
    _____
    _____ *(your mission)*.

- **State a passionate reason for your work.**

Your passion lives within you. You can outwardly express it with an energetic force that causes you to feel an emotion of psychological well-being, like happiness, self-realization, personal growth and intentionality.

Your passion becomes your identity. Your listeners will need to hear your passion, see your passion, and believe in your words. 'Passion' is defined as a strong inclination toward a self-defining activity that you like or love and is willing to invest time and energy on a regular basis. Why do you do this?

Example:
   I intend to teach beginning entrepreneurs and side hustlers how to effectively speed network and sell their products and services in everyday situations.

Brainstorm your thoughts. What is the passion that fuels your business?

Write it here.

I intend to _____

_____

_____ *(passionate reason for your work).*

- **Use words that paint a picture in the listener's mind.**

What do you want your listener to remember about you, your products or services? Add an auditory business detail like "sizzling hot ideas," "hammering out ideas" or "listen to my banging Podcast." These words bring up sounds in the listener's mind.

Workbook: Step 3—Why I Do This

Create a quick visual impression like "floating to the top of the sales charts," "Waistline melting away" or "High-energy videos." These words produce impactful images.

Use sensory words like "mouth-watering smoothies," "rough draft to a smooth read" or "Soft touch solutions." These words awaken your sense of texture.

As you paint your picture with words, say what it is like.

It is like _____
_____
_____*(use words that paint a picture)*.

Step 4—Add Value

The value you add should solve a problem, big or small, that your listener is having based on interactions within the conversation and what you have observed about your listener.

"Add Value" can also be a method to find commonalities between you and your listener. You might discover that you have other subjects, interests, or activities in common. The smallest commonality will open up an opportunity for you to remove one layer of uncertainty. You will give more support and get more support when you increase your comfort level with each other. With each follow-up interaction, another layer of uncertainty melts away.

To create your "Add Value" statement, the following key elements are needed:

- What value do I give?

- Give a website, app, free offer, or something to share.

- Make an introduction to someone or something new for your listener.

- Make a referral for a potential client to your listener, if possible.

Workbook: Step 4—Add Value

Each of the key elements will be explained. I have provided examples to assist you with exploring and completing each of the key elements.

- **What value do I give?**

The most important business value you give is what you sell as your products or services. The relationship value you give is the impression you want to leave in the person's mind. What do you want said about you after you walk away from your networking interaction?

Examples and suggestions for Add Value:

- If you have a product, give a small sample, if possible.
- If you are a coach, give a short coaching session.
- If you are an author, give an excerpt or a chapter of your book.
- Demonstrate a new, simple way to use smart phone technology.
- Share a resource you use in your business.
- Recommend an audio book that helped you.
- Recommend a YouTube channel or video you like.

Speed Networking

I _____
_____ *(what value you give).*

- **Give a website, app, free offer, or something to share**.

Definitely give your business website and all your social media identities. Also, suggest other websites that might benefit your listener.

As the saying states, "The most important things in life are free," so if appropriate, have a free offer prepared for your ideal clients. Be selective with your offers and make sure they add value.

Remember, always be intentional and purposeful during networking. Sharing one meaningful and beneficial resource with your listener could impact your business greatly.

_____
_____ *(website, app, free something to share).*

- **Make an introduction to someone or something new for your listener.**

Suggestions for success:

▶ It is easier to introduce other people to each other than it is for you to introduce yourself to new people.

Workbook: Step 4—Add Value

- When you introduce others, the same will be done for you.

- Think about how you want to be introduced and practice it over and over.

- You will need to teach people how to introduce you. They will learn directly from your self-introduction.

_____ (make an introduction). _____

Continue to Add Value: Prepare a list of business related items you have recently learned about and liked. Examples: Internet business leaders, business concepts, teachable moments in movies, free ebooks, side hustlers with products, specific food items in restaurants, Facebook groups, and meet up groups.

Your networking time will be short and fast paced. Effective communication is usually scripted.

- **Make a referral for a potential client to your listener, if possible.**

A referral is the best compliment a business can receive. A video or written testimonial is even better after purchasing a product or service. You have the power to make or break someone's business or services just by speaking, writing, liking or rating your experience. Building relationships build businesses. Networking will increase your chances of getting free advertisement from people you meet when you are authentic, sincere, and help others reach their business goals.

_____ *(make a referral).*

Step 5—My Contact Information

To create your "Share My Contact Information" statement, the following key elements are needed:

- **Express your gratitude about the interaction.**
- **Ask for permission to connect.**
- **Follow-up on promises, if necessary.**

Each of the key elements will be explained. I have provided examples to assist you with exploring and completing each of the key elements.

- **Express your gratitude about the interaction**

Immediately after meeting someone, and engaging in a brief conversation, show gratitude for the time you have spent with them.

Examples of gratitude.

- ▶ Thank you for speaking with me. I really enjoyed our time together.

- ▶ I have learned so much in my short time with you, thank you.

- ▶ It was nice meeting you. Your business will do well. Thank you for sharing your ideas.

- ▶ I really enjoyed meeting you and getting to know about you and your business.

- **Ask for permission to connect**

This step might be difficult for you. Everyone you network with might not feel the need to stay in contact with you. That's normal. Speed Networking is about you selling yourself and your business to your listener. In sales, perceived rejection happens frequently in the form of a "No" or "Oh, that's okay, not now." Get ready for it. It will happen. Show gratitude for the moment and move on.

If your intuition is whispering to you, "This person is more interested in me romantically than my business," you can politely say, "I will connect with you on social media." Show gratitude for the moment and move on.

Workbook: Step 5—My Contact Information

Examples of professional connections:

- I would like to stay in touch. Please add my number to your cell phone.

- May I text my business card to you?

- What is the best way to stay in contact with you?

- If phone numbers cannot be exchanged, ask to connect on a social media platform or website and then go to your smart phone and connect immediately.

- Invite the listener to your website to connect by leaving their contact information.

- You can text a link to your website for convenience. The least amount of effort in this situation gets quicker connections.

- **Follow-up on promises, if necessary**

In business building and in sales, nothing happens until the follow-up happens. It is important to follow-up with every interaction, even if it is a short response. Your follow-up reassures people you are engaged, capable and interested in building a business relationship. At this point in The 5-Step Speed Networking Method, you are building your credibility with your ideal clients. You are on your journey of selling your products or services.

Ideas for appropriate follow-up:

- Text messages are quick and short. You can add links in the text messages to further connect or add additional value.

- Emails are excellent. You can add people to your products and services email list for future selling opportunities.

- Telephone calls are the deepest way to connect. First, text an inquiry message to set up an appointment to call. Then, you will follow-through in a timely manner.

- Arrange a face-to-face cyber meeting using technology.

- Schedule an in-person discovery meeting to determine how you can support each other's businesses.

The 5 Step-Speed Networking Method

Congratulations! You have successfully completed each session of The 5 Step-Speed Networking Method. Put all of your answers in one continuous dialogue. Fill in your networking dialogue. Save this to your phone, iPad, tablet and computer.

Workbook: Step 5—My Contact Information

Hello, my name is _____
I am a *(use an authentic adjective)* _____
_____ *(tell what you do for whom)* ___
_____
_____ *(state what you created in one sentence)*.

I work with _____ *(your ideal client)* to _____
_____ *(service or product you have)* _____
_____ *(what it will do)* _____
(the transformation, change, or improvement).

I believe that_____
_____
_____*(your mission)*.
I intend to _____ _____
_____*(passionate reason for your work)*. It is like _____
_____
(use words that paint a picture).

I_____
_____ *(what value you give)*. _____
_____*(website, app, free something to share)*. _____
(make an introduction). _____
_____ *(make a referral)*.

I really enjoyed meeting you and discussing _____ *(express your gratitude about the interaction)*. I would like to stay connected. May I text my business card to you *(ask for permission to connect)*? I will be in touch soon *(follow-up promise)*.

> ***You are now certified to Speed Network and sell your products or services by using The 5-Step Speed Networking Method.***

The majority of the participants who began this book and workbook had a Comfort Zone mindset. However, after participants implemented The 5-Step Speed Networking Method, their mindsets shifted to a Forward Thinking mindset. You can do it! Go start brilliant business conversations and grow your business!

> "The meeting of two personalities is like the contact of two chemical substances; if there is any reaction, both are transformed." —Carl Jung, Psychiatrist

For questions and comments, please contact me.
Cynthia@DCSpeedNetworking.com

Visit me online at DCSpeedNetworking.com

Network with me on Twitter:
@DCspeednetwork
@IAmCyMartin

Connect with me on Facebook:
DCSpeedNetworking

www.ingramcontent.com/pod-product-compliance
Lightning Source LLC
Chambersburg PA
CBHW021130300426
44113CB00006B/360